I Wish To Give Sadaqah (Charity), But I'm Broke

-

Jack's Curated Business Idea

-

Jack Lookman

I Wish To Give Sadaqah (Charity), But I'm Broke.

Jack's Curated Business Idea

Copyright © 2024 Jack Lookman Limited

All rights reserved.
No portion of this book may be reproduced in whole or in part, in any form or by any means, electronic or mechanical including photocopying, recording, or by any information storage and retrieval system, without the consent and written permission from the author.

A. ACKNOWLEDGEMENT

I remain eternally grateful to my Creator and Sustainer, for known and unknown favors, blessings, goodness and protection.

I appreciate my parents, for being my vehicle of success.

I was fortified with spiritual and academic knowledge and practices; as well as great life skills to sojourn life.

Contributions of John Tosin Adekunle and are much appreciated.

I appreciate my siblings, who've supported me directly and indirectly.

My beautiful Tolu, Mayowa and Tobi you are very much appreciated.

I appreciate all my Teachers, both formal and informal - Thank you very much.

To all those who've added value to me in one way or the other, I say, thank you.

To my Creator and Sustainer: Alhamdu lillahi rabbi alAAalameena.

To God be the glory.

B. DEDICATION

This piece of work is dedicated to all my family members:

My Late Dad - Bolaji Carew

My Mum - Karimat Carew

My Siblings - Folabi, Taiwo, Kehinde and Titi

My Children - Tolu, Mayowa and Tobi

Ire awawa ri o. (May you find the blessings that you desire)

Ire aje'n jetan (May our Creator and Sustainer grant us everlasting blessings)

Ire Gbankobi (I wish you great unexpected and unexplainable blessings).

May Allah grant us goodness in this world and the hereafter and protect us from the torment of the grave and hell fire. Ameen.

May Allah grant us immeasurable blessings.

C. CONTENT

A. ACKNOWLEDGEMENT
3

B. DEDICATION
4

C. CONTENT
5

D. Preamble
8

1. Inspiration
9

2. What is Charity?
9

3. How can you give sadaqah?
10

4. How will you do this?
11

5. The Process
11

6. Benefits
12

7. Funding
13

8. Naming Your Product
13

9. Team
14

10. Why do you want to give charity?
15

11. Do you need to show your face?
15

12. Format Of Your Content
16

13. On what platforms will my content be?
16

14. How will you monetize?
17

15. Legalities
17

16. Do you need a good voice to execute the projects?
18

17. Target Audience
18

18. Budgetary Considerations
19

19. Could you have variants of the products?
19

20. How Could you Scale the Business?
20

21. Could this be a side hustle or full-time job?
21

22. How much do you need to spend on marketing?
21

23. Marketing Plan
22

24. Exit Strategy
23

25. What resources are required for this business?
23

26. Costing And Pricing Considerations
24

27. Should you create individual or multiple videos
24

28. Checks and Balances
24

29. How could you share your profit?
25

30. Conclusion
26

31. Disclaimer
28

32. Value?
29

Thank you very much for your time. I hope that you got some value. If so, please consider liking, sharing, subscribing, reposting, commenting and following.
29

This is Jack Lookman signing off.
29

33. Useful hashtags
29

34. Useful Links:
30

35. Feedback
31

36. Mission
31

37. Will you like to collaborate?
32

38. Will you like to be mentored by Jack Lookman?
32

39. OTHER PUBLICATIONS BY Jack Lookman Limited
32

40. About Jack Lookman
34

D. Preamble

Most people have great intentions.

To add value to themselves, others, and society.

Some get drowned in life's challenges, difficulties, complexities and distractions.

They end up losing the original desire.

You may say, in other words, 'that as they approached the solution, the forgot the question.'

This content is a little suggestion and wake up call, to make the seemingly impossible, become possible.

Have a great read.

Don't forget to take notes; and to capture the thoughts and creativity presented.

Hello, greetings to one and all. This is Jack Lookman. Welcome to our series, [Jack's Curated Business Ideas](). Today's topic is:

'I wish to give Sadaqah (Charity), but I am broke.'

1. Inspiration

Some people like to give charity; to empower others, to feed the needy, to help victims of conflict, to help family and friends, make a positive difference to society, etc.

The problem, is however, that they probably languish in poverty.

Some of them work but earn very little. They are not exposed to opportunities, or probably have the wrong mindset about earning great incomes, etc.

- As a content creator
- A religious person
- An entrepreneur
- An ex-asalatu (prayer group) member
- And ex-asalatu official, etc.

I see a gap, hence this content.

2. What is Charity?

Muslims call it *Sadaqah* or *Zakat,* Christians call it charity. This is usually a voluntary, non-refundable gift to a third party. It could be:

- Monetary
- Food or drink
- Knowledge
- A Smile
- Sharing your physical strength
- Empathy
- Gadget or physical gift
- Positive emotions
- Sharing beneficial knowledge,
- Etc.

For the purpose of this content, we shall be talking about financial charity and we shall be talking about sadaqah.

3. How can you give sadaqah?

If you have a phone, as well as an internet connection, you could monetize a social media platform and make money. The money could make you financially stable; but more importantly you could give out sadaqah in the form of money and beneficial knowledge. You could also give as sadaqah jariyah, and possibly improve your knowledge of the deen.

Sadaqah jariyah is a gift which yields long-term returns even after you are dead and gone.

4. How will you do this?

- You could record dhikr
- You could record prayers
- You could record Quranic recitations
- You could record good deeds
- You could record beneficial knowledge
- You could record valuable content
- You could have a podcast
- These could be done by you alone, or you could collaborate with third parties

5. The Process

Let's take the YouTube channel or YouTube platform as an example.

- You could register on YouTube for free, thereby getting a YouTube channel.
- Give consideration to the name of your channel.
- You could however rebrand as necessary at later dates
- Create the content

- Market it
- Monetize the channel and then share the profits between your team—yourself and charitable courses
- Replicate the process
- Become good at your doing
- Reinvest and scale your business as necessary
- You could scale to other social media platforms and explore other niches of choice
- You could also explore translations and other content formats, such as books, blogs, etc.

6. Benefits

- You could create wealth
- You could create jobs
- You could give to charity
- You could share beneficial knowledge
- You could increase your beneficial knowledge
- You could become an expert
- You could empower and inspire others
- You could learn new skills
- You could earn sadaqah jariyah (that benefits you after your demise)
- Etc

7. Funding

To fund this project, you could:

- Crowdfund
- Seek sponsors
- Get investors
- Get a loan
- Leverage family and friends
- Collaborate with others
- Etc

8. Naming Your Product

You should consider:

- A short and sharp name
- A memorable name
- A name that relates to what you are offering
- You could research best practices
- See how your competitors have named their products or services
- Carry out research on YouTube, Google or Social media, etc.

- Also ensure that the competition with the chosen name is minimal.
- If you choose a very competitive name your product may end up being drowned in the internet. For example, if you use a name such as *Islam*, your product may not be found because there'll probably be too many searches with that name directly or indirectly.
- Also consider the use of a short phrase rather than a word
- You could also consider branding and using the same identity on different platforms

9. Team

- You may consider doing this project alone or getting a team to complement and multiply your efforts and skill base
- You may require a Video Editor
- Search Engine Optimisation lead
- Content Creator
- A Marketer
- An Entrepreneur
- A Researcher
- A Quality Controller
- A Profit Sharing Formula App lead

- A Legal lead
- A Writer
- A Social Media Manager

10. Why do you want to give charity?

If you're a good and practicing Muslim the reasons to give may be many.

You may wish to:

- Show empathy
- Make impact
- Get rewards from Allah
- Make a positive difference
- Help the sufferers
- Add value to society
- You may wish to give sadaqah jariyah — whose benefits could be long-lasting.
- Etc

11. Do you need to show your face?

You may choose to show or not to show your face; either or both is optional. If creating videos, you could choose to have text or other background pictures as alternatives to showing your face.

12. Format Of Your Content

- This could be text, audio or video
- It could be with subtitles in Arabic, English or other languages of choice
- You might have different variations of each content
    - Some may be in Arabic with English translations; this could also be extended to other languages of choice
- Audio or video content could be looped or automatically repeated, e.g. 11 times, 33 times, 100 times, etc.
- This could also be as Facebook reels or YouTube shorts, etc.
- Your content could be short or long or both

13. On what platforms will my content be?

- You could choose one or multiple platforms
- Suggestions are: different social media platforms, such as YouTube, Facebook, TikTok, Instagram, etc.
- You may also decide to do paperbacks by leveraging Amazon
- You may decide to have a blog/s, podcast/s, etc
- You may decide to do eBooks

14. How will you monetize?

On Social media

- There are different monetization models
- You could do Affiliate Marketing
- You could be sponsored to market different brands
- You could monetize the platforms once you reach certain metrics
- You could promote your other products and services
- If your content is on paperback, you could market and sell this via your social media platforms.
- If you are good at what you do, you could attract business collaborators
- To monetize your YouTube channel for example, you could tell YouTube to show ads before, during and after your YouTube videos. I suggest before and after, so that your audience could enjoy a great listening experience.

15. Legalities

- You may consider putting legalities in place to minimize or avoid conflict; this could include agreements or contracts between concerned parties and stakeholders.
- Any necessary disclaimers and protection of intellectual rights as necessary

- Exit strategies
- Conflict Management
- Fraud prevention and mitigation
- Etc.

16. Do you need a good voice to execute the projects?

- If you'll be doing the recitals yourself, a good audible voice will be a great asset.
- Alternatively, you could get others with these qualities to do the job
- You could either pay them off or engage them as collaborators
- You could then use the Profit Sharing Formula App as a tool to guide the profit-sharing process.

17. Target Audience

- Muslims
- Religious Minds
- Spiritual Minds
- Muslims from different ethnicities
- Youths
- Teenagers

- Adults
- Global audience
- A combination of the above

18. Budgetary Considerations

- Digital device/s
- Your team (or just yourself)
- YouTube channel
- Social media channel
- Marketing
- Research and development
- Free tools for Search Engine Optimization or for keyword research.
- Etc.

19. Could you have variants of the products?

- Yes, you could. For instance, you could have repetitions, for example 11 times, 33 times, 100 times etc — different variants of these.
- For each version you could have the dhikr as standalone
- Or you could complement them with other content niches

- You could also have verbal translations included
- You could have subtitles in Arabic alone or you could include translations in different languages of choice
- Ditto for Quranic recitations
- You could have a collection of beautiful Athaans (calls to prayer)
- You could have a collection of Islamic lectures
- You could have a collection of authentic Hadith's
- You could have moral content that could transcend different spiritual barriers
- Etc.

20. How Could you Scale the Business?

- You could repeat the process for different dhikr
- For different Quranic recitations
- You could create content in different Islamic niches
- You could create content on moral topics
- You could create content on empowerment and inspiration
- You could create content on other areas of interest
- You could create content on other platforms e.g. on other social media platforms, blogs, paperbacks, podcasts, membership sites, etc.

- You could also do public speaking
- You could do mentoring
- You could create courses on membership sites to educate your audience on Islam and other areas of interest
- You could also have your content translated to other languages of choice
- Etc.

21. Could this be a side hustle or full-time job?

- It depends on you and your circumstance
- Good practice is that you start small
- Learn from the experience
- Put systems and structures in place
- And then grow big.
- In other words, you may start as a side hustle and then progress onto a full hustle

22. How much do you need to spend on marketing?

It depends on different factors; for example:

- Your budget
- Your marketing platforms

- The traction to your content
- Your marketing strategy
- Funding
- Your target audience
- Your popularity
- Etc.
- You may spend little or nothing initially and later reinvest to spend much more

23. Marketing Plan

- You need to have a marketing plan
- A marketing budget
- To know on which platforms you intend to market
- Your target audience also needs to be known
- You need to monitor the success of each marketing campaign
- You need to increase the marketing budget for areas where the campaigns are most successful or effective; and reduce the budget on non-performing campaigns.
- You also need to have a marketing timetable
- And also to decide on whether to do the marketing yourself or whether to outsource it to others
- Etc.

24. Exit Strategy

Firstly, you need to know what the exit strategy is.

In simple terms, it's your strategy for when yourself or stakeholders wish to terminate their association with the product or service.

This could include reasons like:

- Conflict
- Death
- Sickness
- Or voluntary resignation

- By having a strategy in place, it reduces or avoids chaos
- It becomes a measured and more manageable process
- And could likely cause less pain

25. What resources are required for this business?

- This could include a digital device/s
- Internet connection
- Relevant skills
- Relevant content
- A team (as necessary)

- Marketing
- Suitable Social media channels
- Or relevant other platforms

26. Costing And Pricing Considerations

- Digital device/s
- Internet connection
- Freelancer/s as necessary
- Search engine optimization tools (as necessary)
- Marketing (as necessary)
- You also need to factor in your profit

27. Should you create individual or multiple videos

- If you are using a platform such as YouTube, you could create multiple videos.
- Your audience could listen to them individually or collectively
- In order to offer the videos for collective listening, you could create playlists, etc.

28. Checks and Balances

- As you embark on your entrepreneurial journey, you need to put checks and balances in place
- You need to protect intellectual rights
- You need to avoid plagiarism
- You need to minimize or avoid conflict
- You need to effectively manage sickness, absence or death of stakeholders, collaborators, freelancers etc.
- You need to carry out due diligence as necessary
- If you've promised particular deliverables to your audience, you need to follow through on these, or manage such situations effectively.

29. How could you share your profit?

- You could consider less fortunate family and friends
- You could consider charity organizations
- You could consider Muslim organizations
- You could consider collaborations in empowering and inspiring the less fortunate
- You could consider contributing to Mosques
- You could consider those affected by conflict and wars, through charity organizations
- You could consider the needy and poor
- You could consider scholarships for the less fortunate, either through scholarships to regular educational

institutions, or online educational institutions, or online courses
- You could consider becoming a philanthropist
- You could consider carrying out community projects
- You could consider adding value to society
- You could improve the quality of life of disabled citizens
- Etc.

30. Conclusion

In conclusion, you could carry out this business model with:
- Little capital
- A smartphone or digital device
- And an internet connection
- Along with content and a social media platform, you are actually good to go
- You could do the business as a solo effort or leverage collaborations
- In case you require funding; this could be got via different options. It could be via:
    - crowdfunding,
    - collaborators
    - family and friends
    - investors

- - loans
  - etc.
- In order to share profits or equity fairly with collaborators you might consider leveraging the Profit Sharing Formula App
- If you require training on carrying out the business you could:
- Book A Chat With Jack Lookman
- Or do the relevant research on the internet, such as YouTube.
- You could also purchase relevant courses on platforms such as Udemy.com
- Please see tips on saving money on our website just go to Jacksempowerment.com and search for Udemy.
  - You could possibly save over 50% of the cost of each online course or courses
- To answer the original topic's intention
- This content should empower in so many ways.
- In addition to your original intention, you could:
  - Earn a decent income for yourself
  - You could become an entrepreneur
  - You could become an influencer
  - You could gain several skills

- You could give out to charity in very sustainable manners
- You could empower and inspire similar minds
- you could create wealth and create jobs
- You could do a lot of dawah through your platforms
- The difference you make to society and individuals could elevate your status (in the duniyah and akhirah, Inshaa Allahu) (in this life and the hereafter, by God's grace.)
- There could be room for collaborative pursuits with third parties
- The experience could catapult you to do even greater things
- Apart from empowering and inspiring others, you could also become empowered and inspired
- And of course the list could go on.

31. Disclaimer

A. At Jack Lookman Limited we do Affiliate Marketing, and make a commission for purchased items through our Affiliate Marketing links, at no additional cost to you.

B. This content is an academic one, based on experience, knowledge, creativity and other considerations.

It's merely an idea, and doesn't guarantee financial success; even though it has great potential to do so.

It's a Curated Business Idea which could stimulate your thoughts and creativity.

You're expected to modify it to suit your business needs to achieve success.

There are many determining factors, for financial success to be achieved. You are expected to carry out due diligence before embarking on any entrepreneurial pursuits.

We wish you immense success as you journey through.

32. Value?

Thank you very much for your time. I hope that you got some value. If so, please consider liking, sharing, subscribing, reposting, commenting and following.

This is Jack Lookman signing off.

   Ire o (I wish you blessings)

   Ire Kabiti (I wish you great blessings)

33. Useful hashtags

#jackscuratedbusinessidea

#jackscuratedbusinessideas

#ireo

#Irekabiti

#JackLookman

#OlayinkaCarew

#CuratedBusinessIdea

#CuratedBusinessIdeas

#empoweringandinspiringgenerations

#EmpowermentandInspiration

34. Useful Links:

Jack Lookman Limited - jacklookmanlimited.com

Book A Chat With Jack Lookman - jacksempowerment.com

Business Collaboration With Jack Lookman - jacksempowerment.com

Jack's Mentoring 101 - jacksempowerment.com

Social media platforms - jacklookmanlimited.com

Jack Lookman's Books - jacklookmanlimited.com

Jack's Curated Business Ideas - jacksempowerment.com

Becoming Organised - jacksempowerment.com

Jack Lookman's Websites : jacklookmanlimited.com

Join Our Community : **Facebook: Jack Lookman**

Udemy And I : jacksempowerment.com

Youtube channel : Curated Business Ideas

35. Feedback

These are my thoughts on this Curated Business Idea. I hope you find them beneficial. If you wish to explore this further, please contact us via "Book A Chat With Jack Lookman".

Also please share this content with those that may benefit therefrom.

36. Mission

Our mission at Jack Lookman Limited is to empower and Inspire Generations by leveraging the internet.

At Jack Lookman Limited
- We create content
- We publish books
- We mentor
- We do affiliate marketing
- We do business collaborations
- And app development collaborations

- We've authored and published several books on

- Curated Business Ideas
- Mindset
- Poetry
- Jaaloo Puzzles
- Yoruba
- Etc

37. Will you like to collaborate?

Does the Jack Lookman brand resonate with you? Will you like to collaborate? If yes, please send an email to: info@jacklookmanlimited.com

Use an appropriate subject heading and narrative.

38. Will you like to be mentored by Jack Lookman?

If yes, please send an email to: info@jacklookmanlimited.com

Use an appropriate subject heading and narrative.

39. OTHER PUBLICATIONS BY Jack Lookman Limited

1. *Despair, Submission, Faith and Hope – Volume 1*
2. *Despair, Submission, Faith and Hope – Volume 2*
3. *Monetising Digital Book Reviews*
4. *E-Commerce For Traditional African Attires*

5. Basic Management And Fundraising Tip For Community Groups

6. Monetising A Digital Library

7. Ajo, The App And Opportunities

8. Empowering Orphans, Widows and Widowers

9. Submission, Gratitude, Faith and Hope

10. Oro Ishiti- Indelible Yoruba Words - Adebanji Osanyingbemi

11. Eid Monetisation by Leveraging Technology

12. What are your thoughts? What is your mindset? - Volume 1

13. What are your thoughts? What is your mindset? - Volume 2

14. Twenty Curated Business Ideas - Volume 1

15. Jaaloo Puzzles - Volume 1

16. Jaaloo Puzzles - Volume 2

17. Beauty Of The Storm - Gabriel Adeola

18. Digital Career Guidance App

19. Bath Sponge Project

20. Community Group Monetisation

21. Profit Sharing Formula App

22. Event Discount App

23. Leasing Digital Tablets / Gadgets To Undergraduates

24. Monetising Jollof Rice

25. Monetising And Empowering The Nigerian Driver

26. Business Idea Critique

27. Remarkable Lessons From Mothers-In-Law - Jumoke Carew

28. Monetising Life Experience

29. Empowering The Less Educated

30. The Bachelors' Club

31. Could You Create Online Schools?

40. About Jack Lookman

Olayinka Carew, aka Jack Lookman is the 1st of 5 Children.
He has 3 children, and an elderly mum. He is resident in the United Kingdom and is of Nigerian origin.

He studied at King's College, Lagos and University of Lagos.
He has varied life and work experiences.
He has been involved in voluntary and paid jobs.
He is dedicating the rest of his life to empowering and inspiring generations.
This is one of his legacy projects.
Though he has health challenges, he does not let that impede his mission and vision.
Even though he studied Engineering in University; his calling is so many miles away from that. He is currently an Entrepreneur, Content Creator, Affiliate Marketer, Volunteer, Business Collaborator and Mentor.

He is the Director and Owner of Jack Lookman Limited, a registered business in the United Kingdom; and their aim is to empower and inspire generations by leveraging the internet.

www.ingramcontent.com/pod-product-compliance
Lightning Source LLC
Chambersburg PA
CBHW030103230526
45471CB00003B/1238